THEOLOGY OF THE BODY
ROSARY
MEDITATIONS

Contemplating Christ's Love for His Bride the Church

Debbie Staresinic

Ruah Woods
PRESS

In accord with the Code of Canon Law, I hereby grant the *Imprimatur* ("Permission to Publish") regarding the manuscript entitled *Theology of the Body: Rosary Meditations*.

> Most Reverend Dennis M. Schnurr
> Archbishop of Cincinnati
> Archdiocese of Cincinnati
> Cincinnati, Ohio
> June 23, 2017

ISBN: 978-1-947008-00-7
Library of Congress Control Number: 2017905065

Excerpts from *Man and Woman He Created Them*, by M. Waldstein, Copyright © Copyright © 2006, M. Waldstein. Used by permission of Pauline Books & Media, 50 St. Paul's Avenue, Boston, MA 02130. All rights reserved.

Excerpts from Vatican Documents adapted with permission of the © LIBRERIA EDITRICE VATICANA.

Excerpts from the English translation of the *Catechism of the Catholic Church* for use in the United States of America Copyright © 1994, United States Catholic Conference, Inc. — Libreria Editrice Vaticana. Used with Permission.

Excerpts from the *Diary of Saint Maria Faustina Kowalska* used with permission of the Marian Fathers of the Immaculate Conception of the Blessed Virgin Mary.

Excerpt from *The Spirit of the Liturgy* by Joseph Cardinal Ratzinger used with permission of Ignatius Press.

The translation of Augustine, *Sermo Suppositus* 120:3 is taken from Pitre, *Jesus the Bridegroom,* p. 93. Meditations for The Wedding Feast at Cana, The Crowning with Thorns and The Crucifixion were also inspired by this book.

Scripture texts in this work are taken from the New American Bible, revised edition © 2010, 1991, 1986, 1970 Confraternity of Christian Doctrine, Washington, D.C. and are used by permission of the copyright owner. All Rights Reserved. No part of the New American Bible may be reproduced in any form without permission in writing from the copyright owner.

Cover photo © *L'Osservatore Romano*. Used with permission.
Cover design and layout: Mike Fontecchio, CatholicDesigner.com

Printed in the United States of America.
Published in the United States by Ruah Woods Press.

Dedicated to my husband Dan,
our children and grandchildren

Contents

Acknowledgments

I thank my heavenly intercessors — the Blessed Virgin Mary, St. Joseph and St. John Paul II — for praying for the guidance of the many people who contributed to this book.

My enduring thanks goes to all whose support has made this book possible. I am grateful to Joan Kingsland, my friend and colleague at Ruah Woods, for her valuable feedback and encouragement throughout this project. Additional thanks to Jen Settle at the Theology of the Body Institute for her helpful comments and suggestions. Particular thanks goes to Steve Deiters and Keith Warnke at Ruah Woods Press for their help with publication. I express my gratitude to Barbara Rose and Stephen Kovacs for their editing expertise. My heartfelt thanks to gifted book designer Mike Fontecchio for making this project come to life in a physical way and for his patience throughout the process. I am grateful to Dr. Brant Pitre and his book *Jesus the Bridegroom*, which was a turning point in the development of this work. Thanks also to Christopher West, faculty member at the Theology of the Body Institute, founder of the Cor Project and the spiritual and intellectual inspiration for much of this book.

Finally, and most importantly, I thank my husband Dan for his loving support throughout this project and his continued example of self-giving love. I am grateful for his constant encouragement to be the best I can be and for the shared experience of helping each other, our children and our grandchildren get to Heaven.

Preface

Numerous popes throughout history have attributed great importance to the Rosary, the "favorite prayer" of St. John Paul II. By choosing *Totus Tuus* (totally yours) as his papal motto and placing his entire pontificate into Mary's hands, St. John Paul II demonstrated the critical importance of devotion to the Mother of Jesus. In his book *Crossing the Threshold of Hope*, the Pope stated that the Church's future victories will come through Mary.

I was introduced to St. John Paul II's Theology of the Body (TOB) in 2011. Because the association between TOB and the Rosary is so powerful, I began to seek a set of Rosary meditations written from a TOB point of view. But there was nothing available.

This book is the result of my effort to satisfy that need. I hope that it leads you to a deeper intimacy and relationship with Jesus Christ and that it sparks a greater appreciation for the beauty and power of TOB. If it does, then I invite you to share it with others.

May the mysteries contained in the Most Holy Rosary serve to illuminate the mysteries of God revealed in the body.

What is Theology of the Body?

Theology of the Body (TOB) is St. John Paul II's teaching on what it means to be human. It explains what it means to be made — male and female — in the image and likeness of God, addressing the questions: Who am I? Why am I here? How do I find happiness?

Through Sacred Scripture and Sacred Tradition, St. John Paul II explains how the body reveals the answer to each of these questions. TOB helps us to grasp our identity, our vocation and our purpose in life.

TOB inspires a deepened awareness of human dignity and reverence for oneself and others. Thereby, we embrace the call to be a gift and to welcome others as gifts. This is how we fulfill the meaning of our existence and experience true love, joy, peace, freedom and happiness.

What is the Rosary?

"The Rosary of the Virgin Mary… is a prayer loved by countless Saints and encouraged by the Magisterium. Simple yet profound, it still remains, at the dawn of this third millennium, a prayer of great significance, destined to bring forth a harvest of holiness…

"Though clearly Marian in character, the Rosary is at heart a Christocentric prayer. In the sobriety of its elements, it has all the *depth of the Gospel message in its entirety*, of which it can be said to be a compendium…

"With the Rosary, the Christian people *sits at the school of Mary* and is led to contemplate the beauty on the face of Christ and to experience the depths of his love. Through the Rosary the faithful receive abundant grace, as though from the very hands of the Mother of the Redeemer."

— St. John Paul II,
The Rosary of the Virgin Mary, no. 1

How to Pray the Rosary

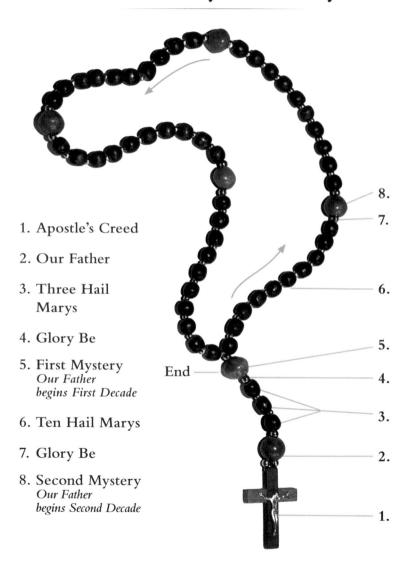

1. Apostle's Creed

2. Our Father

3. Three Hail Marys

4. Glory Be

5. First Mystery
   Our Father
   begins First Decade

6. Ten Hail Marys

7. Glory Be

8. Second Mystery
   Our Father
   begins Second Decade

End

8.

7.

6.

5.

4.

3.

2.

1.

Prayers of the Rosary

Apostles' Creed

I believe in God, the Father Almighty, Creator of Heaven and earth; and in Jesus Christ, His only Son, Our Lord, Who was conceived by the Holy Spirit, born of the Virgin Mary, suffered under Pontius Pilate, was crucified, died, and was buried. He descended into Hell; the third day He arose again from the dead; He ascended into Heaven, and is seated at the right hand of God, the Father Almighty; from thence He shall come to judge the living and the dead. I believe in the Holy Spirit, the holy Catholic Church, the communion of saints, the forgiveness of sins, the resurrection of the body, and life everlasting. Amen.

Our Father

Our Father, Who art in Heaven, hallowed be Thy name. Thy kingdom come. Thy will be done, on earth as it is in Heaven. Give us this day our daily bread. And forgive us our trespasses, as we forgive those who trespass against us. And lead us not into temptation, but deliver us from evil. Amen.

Hail Mary

Hail Mary, full of grace, the Lord is with thee. Blessed art thou among women, and blessed is the fruit of thy womb, Jesus. Holy Mary, Mother of God, pray for us sinners, now, and at the hour of our death. Amen.

Glory Be

Glory be to the Father, and to the Son, and to the Holy Spirit. As it was in the beginning, is now, and ever shall be, world without end. Amen.

Mysteries of the Rosary

Joyful Mysteries *(Suggested: Mondays and Saturdays)*

The Annunciation
The Wedding Proposal and the Word Becomes Flesh

The Visitation
The Bride Shares the Good News

The Nativity
God's Plan for the Human Person is Revealed

The Presentation of the Lord
The Encounter

The Finding of Jesus in the Temple
The Mission of the Bridegroom

Luminous Mysteries *(Suggested: Thursdays)*

The Baptism of the Lord
The Nuptial Bath

The Wedding Feast at Cana
Jesus Assumes the Role of Bridegroom

The Proclamation of the Kingdom
The Wedding Invitation: A Call to Conversion

The Transfiguration
A Glimpse of the Bridegroom's Glorified Body

The Institution of the Eucharist
The Wedding Feast

Sorrowful Mysteries *(Suggested: Tuesdays and Fridays)*

The Agony in the Garden
The Bridegroom Anticipates the Gift

The Scourging at the Pillar
The Scourging of the Bridegroom

The Crowning with Thorns
The Wedding Crown

The Carrying of the Cross
The Bridegroom Carries His Cross

The Crucifixion
The Consummation of the Marriage

Glorious Mysteries *(Suggested: Wednesdays and Sundays)*

The Resurrection
The New Life of the Bridegroom

The Ascension
The Bridegroom Prepares a Place for His Bride

The Descent of the Holy Spirit
The Holy Spirit Prepares the Bride for the Marriage of the Lamb

The Assumption
The Bride Joins Her Spouse

The Coronation of Mary
The Bridegroom Crowns the Bride

THE JOYFUL MYSTERIES

The body, in fact, and only the body, is capable of making visible what is invisible, the spiritual and the divine. It has been created to transfer into the visible reality of the world the mystery hidden from eternity in God, and thus to be a sign of it.

— TOB 19:4

THE ANNUNCIATION
The Wedding Proposal and the Word Becomes Flesh

God proposes and promises to bring His Bride into an everlasting union with Him. On behalf of mankind, Mary answers "yes" and the Word becomes flesh. Christ comes to us in the body, making visible the invisible God. This is how the love of God is revealed to the world. God sent His only son into the world in order to bring us into eternal union with Him.

All of creation is a visible sign of the invisible reality of God. The human body in fact reveals the deepest mysteries of God and humanity. Man and woman, the crown of creation, image God most fully in their call to union. It is good to ponder this, to be in awe and filled with gratitude toward our Creator.

Voices of the Church

As Mary stood before the Lord, she represented the whole of humanity. In the angel's message, it was as if God made a marriage proposal to the human race. And in our name, Mary said yes. (Pope Benedict XVI, Angelus address, 20 July 2008)

Prayer

Lord, help me to be moved with wonder and gratitude for the gift of the Incarnation and all of creation. Amen.

Philippe De Champaigne, The Visitation, 1643-48

The human body… contains "from the beginning"… the power to express love: precisely that love in which the human person becomes a gift and — through this gift — fulfills the very meaning of his being and existence.

— TOB 15:1

THE VISITATION

The Bride Shares the Good News

Already in Mary's womb, the union of God and humanity has begun. Mary makes a gift of herself by traveling to the hill country to share the good news with her cousin Elizabeth. We too are called to proclaim the good news of our invitation to the Eternal Wedding Feast.

The Visitation is a reminder of our primary vocation to love. Our calling in life is to love as God loves. We do this by becoming self-gift. This is the meaning of our existence. God in His very essence, Father, Son and Holy Spirit, is self-gift. Made in His image, self-gift is our essence too. We are called to give ourselves to Him and to one another.

Voices of the Church

God is not solitude, but perfect communion. For this reason the human person, the image of God, realizes himself or herself in love, which is a sincere gift of self. (Pope Benedict XVI, Angelus address, Solemnity of the Most Holy Trinity, 22 May 2005)

Prayer

Lord, inspire me to look for opportunities throughout the day to make a gift of myself to others. Amen.

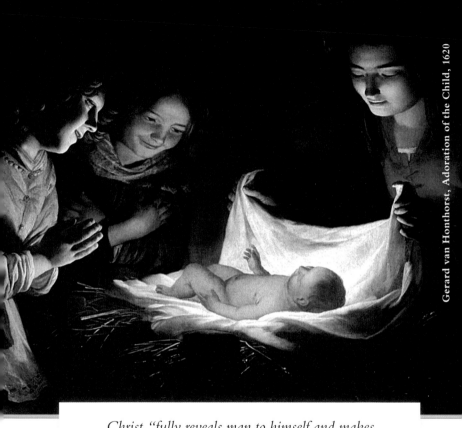

Gerard van Honthorst, Adoration of the Child, 1620

Christ *"fully reveals man to himself and makes his supreme calling clear"* GS 22:1.

— TOB 86:8

THE NATIVITY

God's Plan for the Human Person is Revealed

As we contemplate the Infant Jesus, we come to know the true face of God and the true face of man. God took on a body and became man in order to communicate His own life to us and to answer the question "Who is man?" It is only in light of Jesus that the mystery of the human person becomes manifest. The more we come to know Jesus, the more we understand our creation as male and female and our call to union with Him and one another.

Voices of the Church

On that Holy Night, in taking flesh God wanted to make a gift of himself to men and women, he gave himself for us; God made his Only Son a gift for us, he took on our humanity to give his divinity to us. This is the great gift... In that Child, the Son of God contemplated at Christmas, we can recognize the true face not only of God but also of the human being; and only by opening ourselves to his grace and seeking to follow him every day do we fulfil God's plan for us, for each one of us. (Pope Benedict XVI, General Audience, 9 January 2013)

Prayer

Lord, deepen my desire to spend time with You so I can come to know You and all that You have planned for me. Amen.

Giuseppe Marchesi, The Presentation in the Temple, c. 1732–44

Man becomes an image of God not so much in the moment of solitude as in the moment of communion.

— TOB 9:3

THE PRESENTATION OF THE LORD

The Encounter

Mary and Joseph bring Jesus to the Temple. This is the first encounter between Jesus and His people, represented by Simeon and Anna. Jesus is at the center and draws all of them to the Father's house. Similarly, Jesus comes to us. He draws us to the Temple, the Church. We encounter Him, take Him into our arms and bring Him to others.

We exist in an intricate web of relationships and are intrinsically related to one another. Created in God's image, each and every person has great dignity and is worthy of our respect. The fruits are marvelous when this awareness imbues and enlivens our relationships with others.

Voices of the Church

No man is an island, entire of itself. Our lives are involved with one another, through innumerable interactions they are linked together. No one lives alone. No one sins alone. No one is saved alone. The lives of others continually spill over into mine: in what I think, say, do and achieve. And conversely, my life spills over into that of others: for better and for worse. (Pope Benedict XVI, *Spe Salvi*, 2007)

Prayer

Lord, help me to see the image of God in others and to treat each person with the utmost respect. Amen.

José de Avelar Rebelo, *Christ Among the Doctors*, c. 1635

The redemption of man and the world (and thus precisely of the "redemption of the body")... is, in fact, the perspective of the whole gospel, of the whole teaching, even more, of the whole mission of Christ.

— TOB 49:3

THE FINDING OF JESUS IN THE TEMPLE

The Mission of the Bridegroom

Although His role as bridegroom is yet to be revealed, the finding of Jesus in the Temple points to His awareness of His mission. Jesus says, "Did you not know that I must be in my Father's house?" (Lk 2:49). Jesus acknowledges His role to do the Father's work. The Father sent the Son to "restore creation to the purity of its origins" (CCC 2336).

In the Sermon on the Mount, Jesus appeals to the human heart to be pure. Jesus is calling us to a new way of life, a new way of living that goes back to God's original plan. He wants us to be more than mere "rule followers." In Matthew 5:17, Jesus explains that He came "not to abolish the law but to fulfill it." When our hearts are pure, we are free from the law. We no longer need the rules. Purity of heart is possible through God's grace.

Voices of the Church

The law was therefore given, in order that grace might be sought; grace was given, in order that the law might be fulfilled. (St. Augustine, *On the Spirit and the Letter*, Chapter 34)

Prayer

Lord, cultivate in me a desire to allow You to purify my heart and to see as You see. Amen.

THE LUMINOUS MYSTERIES

*Baptism prepares the Bride (Church) for the
Bridegroom. It makes the Church the Bride of Christ.*

— TOB 91:7

The Baptism of the Lord

The Nuptial Bath

In Baptism, the soul becomes the Bride of Christ. It cleanses us from sin and prepares us for the "wedding day." "Baptism... is a nuptial mystery; it is so to speak the nuptial bath that precedes the wedding feast, the Eucharist" (CCC 1617).

As Jesus comes out of the water, the Holy Spirit descends upon Him like a dove, the heavens open and the Father's voice is heard from on high: "You are my beloved Son; with you I am well pleased" (Mk 1:11).

Christ's baptism reveals His divine sonship. This gives us an opportunity to reflect on our own identity as sons and daughters of God. Through the redemption Christ won for us, God forgives us and raises us from the status of slaves to adopted sons and daughters. This is our foundational identity. We are beloved sons and daughters of God before anything else.

Voices of the Church

Baptism is adoption and admission into God's family, into communion with the Most Holy Trinity, into communion with the Father, the Son and the Holy Spirit. (Pope Benedict XVI, Homily, 7 January 2007)

Prayer

Lord, inspire me to contemplate and delight in my identity as a "child of God," given to me in Baptism and merited by You. Amen.

Bartolome Esteban Murillo, The Marriage Feast at Cana, 1675

*For this reason a man will leave his father and his
mother and unite with his wife, and the two will
form one flesh. This mystery is great; I say this with
reference to Christ and the Church Eph 5:31-32…
We should consider this passage as the "crowning" of
the themes and truths that ebb and flow like long waves
through the Word of God revealed in the Scripture.*

— TOB 87:1, 3

THE WEDDING FEAST AT CANA

Jesus Assumes the Role of Bridegroom

By fulfilling His mother's request to provide wine for the wedding, Jesus begins to reveal His identity as Bridegroom.

It is no accident that Jesus performed His first miracle at a wedding. Our creation as male and female and the call of the two to become one flesh reveal the very meaning of human existence. The Sacrament of Marriage is a sign of Christ's love for His bride, the Church. St. Paul links the "one flesh union" of man and woman with the union of Christ and the Church in Ephesians 5:31–32. It is indeed a "great mystery," as St. Paul so profoundly suggests. This analogy, St. John Paul II says, is "the most important point of the whole text, *in some sense its keystone*" (TOB 93:1).

Each Christian, whether single, celibate for the kingdom of God, or sacramentally married, is, as part of the Church, invited to be the Bride of Christ.

Voices of the Church

The Lord shows us that the relationship between Him and the Church is matrimonial. This is the deepest reason why the Church guards the Sacrament of Marriage. (Pope Francis, Homily, 6 September 2013)

Prayer

Lord, give me the eyes to see the mystery of God revealed in my body. Amen.

Carl Heinrich Bloch, Sermon on the Mount, 1877

In the Sermon on the Mount, Christ said "You have heard that it was said, 'You shall not commit adultery.' But I say to you: Whoever looks at a woman to desire her lustfully has already committed adultery with her in his heart" (Mt 5:27-28).

— TOB 24:1

THE PROCLAMATION OF THE KINGDOM

The Wedding Invitation: A Call to Conversion

The Bridegroom announces the Kingdom of God, inviting everyone to the great wedding feast. This proclamation is a joyful one that calls for conversion.

"In the Sermon on the Mount — Christ invites us to overcome concupiscence, even in the exclusively interior movements of the human heart... This hope of victory over sin... is the hope of everyday" (TOB 86:6). It is made possible through the grace of the Holy Spirit. The temporal and eternal fruits of living "according to the spirit" are abundant and include love, joy, peace, forbearance, kindness, goodness, faithfulness, gentleness and self-control. Following Christ does not take away our freedom but instead brings true and lasting happiness.

Voices of the Church

We do not need to wait for the kingdom of God in the future... God comes to establish his lordship in our history, today, every day, in our life; and there — where it is welcomed with faith and humility — love, joy and peace blossom. The condition for entering and being a part of this kingdom is to implement a change in our life, which is to *convert*, to convert every day, to take a step forward each day. (Pope Francis, Angelus address, 4 December 2016)

Prayer

Lord, help me to experience the true freedom and happiness that come from following You. Amen

When we speak about the glorified body through the resurrection to new life, what we have in mind is man, male and female, in all the truth of his humanity, who together with the eschatological experience of the living God (with the vision "face to face") will experience precisely this meaning of his body.

— TOB 69:5

The Transfiguration

A Glimpse of the Bridegroom's Glorified Body

In order to prepare the Apostles for the scandal of the Cross, Jesus strengthened their faith by the Transfiguration. By allowing Peter, James and John to catch a glimpse of His glorified body, Jesus gave them a supernatural perspective on the events yet to unfold.

"In the event of the transfiguration the Father asks us to put our faith in Christ: 'Listen to him.' For the transfiguration that we witness is destined to transfigure us: 'He will change our lowly body to conform with His glorified body'" (*Magnificat*, Fr. Peter John Cameron, OP, Editor, February 2016, p. 312).

Voices of the Church

The Church contemplates the transfigured face of Christ in order to be confirmed in faith and to avoid being dismayed at his disfigured face on the Cross. In both cases, she is the Bride before her Spouse, sharing in his mystery and surrounded by his light. (Pope John Paul II, *Vita Consecrata*, 1996)

Prayer

Lord, awaken me to see Your glory and to be filled with hope in the resurrection. May Your Transfiguration transfigure me. Amen.

Juan de Juanes, The Last Supper, c. 1560

*These two functions of the mutual gift exchange are
deeply connected in the whole process of the "gift
of self": giving and accepting the gift interpenetrate
in such a way that the very act of giving becomes
acceptance and acceptance transforms itself into giving.*

— TOB 17:4

THE INSTITUTION OF THE EUCHARIST

The Wedding Feast

On the night before He suffered on the cross, Jesus shared one last meal with His disciples. "While they were eating, Jesus took bread, said the blessing, broke it, and giving it to his disciples said, 'Take and eat; this is my body'" (Mt 26:26).

Christ was revealing what He would do the next day on the cross. In the Eucharist, Jesus gives His Bride the wedding gift of Himself.

The giving and receiving of the Eucharist interpenetrate in such a way that our acceptance of the Gift transforms itself into the very act of giving. We receive Him and, in exchange, we give ourselves back to Him.

Voices of the Church

In the Eucharist a communion takes place that corresponds to the union of man and woman in marriage. Just as they become "one flesh," so in Communion, we all become "one spirit," one person, with Christ. (Joseph Cardinal Ratzinger, *The Spirit of the Liturgy*, 2014)

Prayer

Lord, help me to receive with reverence the gift of Yourself given to me in the Holy Eucharist and to offer myself to You in return. Amen.

THE SORROWFUL MYSTERIES

Heinrich Hoffman, Christ in Gethsemane, 1886

Christ made a "gift of self" to the Father through
obedience to the point of death on the cross.

— TOB 90:5

THE AGONY IN THE GARDEN

The Bridegroom Anticipates the Gift

In the Garden of Gethsemane, "oppressed by foreknowledge of the trials that await him, Jesus cries out to the Father… and asks Him to take away, if possible, the cup of suffering. But… in order to bring man back to the Father's face, Jesus not only had to take on the face of man, but he had to burden himself with the 'face' of sin" (Pope John Paul II, *Novo Millennio Ineunte*, no. 25).

It is good to contemplate the sacrificial nature of Christ's gift of self to the Father. When we make a gift of ourselves by sacrificing our own needs and desires for the sake of the other, we image Christ and fulfill the meaning of our existence.

Voices of the Church

In Jesus' prayer to the Father on that terrible and marvelous night in Gethsemane… his human will, shaken by fear and anguish, was taken up by his divine will in such a way that God's will was done on earth. And this is also important in our own prayers: we must learn to entrust ourselves more to divine Providence, to ask God for the strength to come out of ourselves to renew our "yes" to him, to say to him "thy will be done," so as to conform our will to his. (Pope Benedict XVI, General Audience, 1 February 2012)

Prayer

Lord, teach me to love like You, by placing the needs of others before my own. Amen.

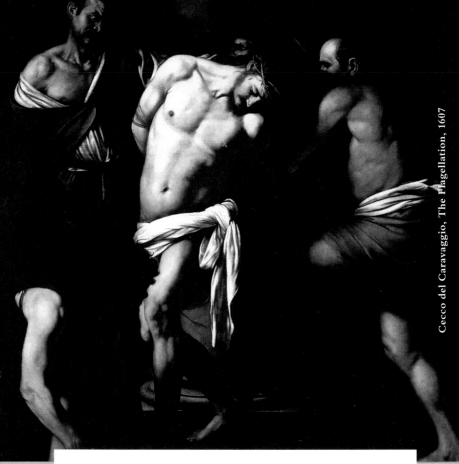

Cecco del Caravaggio, The Flagellation, 1607

Christ appeals to the human heart, exhorting it to purity.
— TOB 59:1

THE SCOURGING AT THE PILLAR

The Scourging of the Bridegroom

At the pillar, Jesus is stripped and tortured with rods and whips. Blood flows forth as hunks of flesh are torn from His body. Jesus offers His excruciating pain and suffering for the sins of mankind.

Purity of heart signifies being free from *every kind* of sin. Our Lord wants us to live fully integrated lives of purity. This includes being pure in mind, body and intention. Purity is a virtue obtained through personal effort. It is also a gift of the Holy Spirit to which we must open ourselves. We cannot achieve it on our own.

The rewards for living a life of purity are great. "The 'pure in heart' are promised that they will see God face to face and be like him" (CCC 2519).

Voices of the Church

Jesus gave me to know for what sins He subjected Himself to the scourging: these are sins of impurity. Oh, how dreadful was Jesus' moral suffering during the scourging! (Maria Faustina Kowalska, *Diary: Divine Mercy in My Soul*, 445)

Prayer

Lord, help me to live a fully integrated life of purity so I can see and be like You. Amen.

Annibale Carracci, *Christ Wearing the Crown of Thorns, Supported by Angels*, 1587

*In this struggle between good and evil, man proves
to be stronger thanks to the power of the Holy
Spirit, who, working within the human spirit,
causes its desires to bear fruit in the good.*

— TOB 51:6

The Crowning with Thorns
The Wedding Crown

According to Jewish scripture and tradition, it was customary for the Jewish bridegroom to wear a crown on his wedding day. Jesus' wedding crown is made of thorns. The Roman soldiers amused themselves at the expense of Jesus. They dressed Him in a purple robe, placed a reed in His hand as if it were a scepter, and drove a crown of thorns into His head, all the while pretending to offer Him homage. This was Satan's "hour."

Jesus endures the agonizing pain of the scourging and the emotional pain of the mockery. The Christian life demands courage. Scripture warns us to "Be sober and vigilant. Your opponent the devil is prowling around like a roaring lion looking for someone to devour. Resist him, steadfast in faith, knowing that your fellow believers throughout the world undergo the same sufferings" (1 Peter 5:8-9). St. Paul describes the interior battle of our inclination to sin, but he also speaks of the redemption at work within each of us.

Voices of the Church

When faced with evil we often have the sensation that we can do nothing, but our prayers are in fact the first and most effective response we can give, they strengthen our daily commitment to goodness. The power of God makes our weakness strong. (Pope Benedict XVI, General Audience, 12 September 2012)

Prayer

Lord, strengthen my will to choose good over evil. Amen.

Hieronymus Bosch, Christ Carrying the Cross, 1516

When the cross is embraced it becomes a sign of love and of total self-giving. To carry it behind Christ means to be united with him in offering the greatest proof of love.

— St. John Paul II, 16th Annual World
Youth Day, 14 February 2001

THE CARRYING OF THE CROSS

The Bridegroom Carries His Cross

The march to Calvary was horrendously painful. Weary from the extreme torture He had already endured, Jesus fell multiple times and was crushed by the weight of the cross. Knowing that Jesus didn't have the strength to carry His cross by Himself, the Roman soldiers ordered Simon of Cyrene to carry it for Him.

Jesus doesn't order us to carry our crosses. He never forces us. Instead, Jesus invites us to follow Him and to carry our crosses with Him. In doing so, we unite ourselves to Him through self-giving love.

Voices of the Church

The Lord then said to me, "The bride must resemble her Betrothed." (Maria Faustina Kowalska, *Diary: Divine Mercy in My Soul*, 268)

Prayer

Lord, help me to embrace my cross and to carry it with You as a sign of my love and total self-giving. Amen.

Diego Velázquez, Christ Crucified, c. 1632

The Church is precisely that body, which... receives from him... the fullness of salvation as a gift of Christ, who "gave himself for her" to the end.

— TOB 90:5

THE CRUCIFIXION

The Consummation of the Marriage

On the cross, Jesus is joined to His Bride, the Church, in an everlasting covenant. The wedding has begun, but it is not yet fully complete. The ultimate union of God and His people will be brought to fulfillment when the Bridegroom returns and takes His Bride with Him.

Christ's saving love is the love of the eternal Bridegroom for His Bride. We are invited to share in this eternal communion with God. This is the central message of the Gospel, the very meaning and purpose of our existence.

Voices of the Church

Like a bridegroom Christ went forth from his chamber.... He came to the marriage-bed of the Cross, and there in mounting it, he consummated his marriage. And when he perceived the sighs of the creature, he lovingly gave himself up to the torment in place of his bride, and joined himself to her forever. (St. Augustine, *Sermo Suppositus*, 120)

Prayer

Lord, prepare me for the ultimate union with You by helping me unite myself to You now, in every aspect of my life. Amen.

THE GLORIOUS MYSTERIES

Cecco del Caravaggio, The Resurrection, 1619

The resurrection clearly affirms that man's ultimate destiny cannot be understood as a state of the soul alone, separated... from the body, but must be understood as the definitively and perfectly "integrated" state of man brought about by... a union of the soul with the body.

— TOB 66:6

THE RESURRECTION
The New Life of the Bridegroom

Jesus' resurrection helps us to understand our own resurrection. Jesus rose bodily. We too will rise bodily. We are embodied spirits. Our bodies are intrinsic to who we are and therefore are deserving of great respect. As St. Paul teaches, our bodies are temples of the Holy Spirit.

Christ brought about redemption for the entire person, including our bodies. In Heaven, our bodies will be fully renewed. There will be no more pain and suffering. There will be perfect harmony between body and spirit. We will be freed from the opposition of what St. Paul refers to in Romans 7:15: "What I do, I do not understand. For I do not do what I want, but I do what I hate." There will be no more battle. We will finally be freed from all the things that are keeping us from loving the way we are intended to love.

We are destined to be raised up and united in love with the Holy Trinity forever. We are sojourners in this world, on our way home to Heaven. It is good to keep this goal in sight. Meditating on it feeds our Christian hope.

Voices of the Church

The hope of the resurrection never fails us. The first one who walked this path was Jesus. We will walk the path he has walked. (Pope Francis, Homily, 2 November 2016)

Prayer

Lord, impress upon me what it means to be an integrated body and soul. Allow that understanding to guide my thoughts and actions. Amen.

Dosso Dossi, The Ascension, 16th c.

Participation in divine nature, participation in the interior life of God himself, penetration and permeation of what is essentially human by what is essentially divine, will then reach its peak, so that the life of the human spirit will reach a fullness that was absolutely inaccessible to it before.

— TOB 67:3

THE ASCENSION

The Bridegroom Prepares a Place for His Bride

During the Last Supper, Jesus announced that He will leave His disciples behind in order to prepare a place for them.

In Heaven, the spousal meaning of the body (our call to union and communion) will be fulfilled. There will be no marriage in Heaven. We will no longer need the visible sign of marriage pointing us to the invisible reality of the heavenly wedding. The transformed life that God has prepared for us is still a human life: body and soul, male or female.

We will see God face to face, and we will participate in the inner life of God Himself. While our participation in the divine nature will not be fully complete until we are with Him in Heaven, we are called to experience an ever increasing unity with Him right here and now, through prayer and the sacraments.

Voices of the Church

Christ ascends into heaven with the humanity he has assumed and which he has resurrected from the dead: that humanity is ours, transfigured, divinized, made eternal. (Pope Benedict XVI, Regina Caeli address, 21 May 2006)

Prayer

Lord, help me to keep my eyes fixed on the glorious vision of You that awaits me in Heaven. Amen.

Tiziano Vecellio, The Descent of the Holy Ghost, c. 1515

In his everyday life, man must draw from the mystery of the redemption of the body the inspiration and the strength to overcome the evil that is dormant in him... What is at stake is the hope of everyday, which in the measure of normal tasks and difficulties of human life helps to overcome "evil with good" (Rom 12:21).

— TOB 86:7

THE DESCENT OF THE HOLY SPIRIT

The Holy Spirit Prepares the Bride
for the Marriage of the Lamb

Although the body's redemption will not be fully realized until the end of time, we are meant to experience a foretaste of redemption even now. This is made possible to us through the power of the Holy Spirit.

The Holy Spirit strengthens us and enables us to give and receive love in accord with the spousal meaning of our bodies. The entire purpose of our life here on earth is to learn to love and be loved as God loves and so prepare ourselves to share in His eternal life. Every day is an opportunity to put this into practice. Our earthly life can be regarded as "marriage prep" for the Eternal Wedding Feast in Heaven.

Each decision we make is an opportunity to grow in holiness, to become more Christ-like and to live out more fully the spousal meaning of our lives. In so doing, we prepare ourselves to experience "what eye has not seen, and ear has not heard, and what has not entered the human heart, what God has prepared for those who love him" (1 Corinthians 2:9).

Voices of the Church

In His final victory over sin and death, the Bridegroom, now risen... desires to purify his Betrothed in expectation of his coming. (Pope Francis, Message for Lent 2016)

Prayer

Lord, fill me with the Holy Spirit so that Your ways become my ways. Amen.

Guido Reni, The Assumption of the Virgin, 1636

"And God saw everything that He had made, and indeed, it was very good" (Gen 1:31). Man appears in the visible world as the highest expression of the divine gift, because he bears within himself the inner dimension of the gift. And with it he carries into the world his particular likeness to God.

— TOB 19:3

THE ASSUMPTION

The Bride Joins Her Spouse

The human person is the crown of creation. Created by God and called to communion with Him, each person is unique and unrepeatable and has great dignity.

Mary "is the representative and archetype of the whole human race" (St. John Paul II, *Mulieris Dignitatem*, 4). Like Mary, we are called to be open to and bear forth divine life. The Assumption of Mary illuminates the goodness of our bodies. God made the body good and desires that it be with Him in Heaven.

Voices of the Church

Mary's Assumption reveals the nobility and dignity of the human body... By looking at her, the Christian learns to discover the value of his own body and to guard it as a temple of God, in expectation of the resurrection. The Assumption, a privilege granted to the Mother of God, thus has immense value for the life and destiny of humanity. (Pope John Paul II, General Audience, 9 July 1997)

Prayer

Lord, help me to discover the value of my body and to guard it as a temple of God. Amen.

Diego Velazquez, The Coronation of the Virgin, c. 1635-36

The absolute and eternal spousal meaning of the glorified body will be revealed in union with God himself, by seeing him "face to face", glorified moreover through the union... that will unite all the "sharers in the other world," men and women, in the mystery of the communion of saints.

— TOB 75:1